Put On a
1, 2, 3

Written by Judy Nayer
Photographs by Elbaliz Mendez

Celebration Press
Parsippany, New Jersey

Do you want to have some fun with your friends? Put on a play!
Here's how to do it in ten easy steps.

2

① Choose the play you want to perform. You can find plays in your library. You can also pick a story you know, like Little Red Riding Hood, and write your own play. Make sure your characters have a lot to do or say!

② Choose people to work on the play. Decide who will play each part. Give each actor a copy of the script. The script contains all the actors' lines.

ABCDEFGHIJKLMNOPQRSTUVWXYZ
1234567890

Little Red Riding
Hood - Becky
F. Michael
dtsman - Tychon
ndma - Stephanie

4

There are lots of other jobs besides acting. Some people can help build the sets. Other people can help make costumes. One person, the director, makes sure the actors, the sets, and the costumes tell the story well.

③ Start rehearsing. First read through the whole play together. Then start to learn the lines you will have to say.

Try to act just like the person, animal, or thing you are pretending to be. Be sure to speak loudly and clearly.

7

4 A play needs a stage. Decide where you are going to put on your play. Could it be at your school? Could it be in your basement or backyard?

(5) It's time to work on the sets for your play. You can paint a background on a large sheet of paper. You can make furniture out of boxes. Use your imagination!

q

(6) Now gather props for your play. Anything that is used by the actors is a prop. It could be food, a basket, or a flower.

 Don't forget costumes. Decide what each character will wear. Maybe you can borrow clothes. Your parents might be able to help sew costumes. Sometimes actors use masks.

8 Does your play need music or sound effects? A sound effect might be birds singing or a knock on the door. You can record them on tape in the right order to play during your production.

Presenting
Little
Red
Riding Hood
Tuesday, June 30
4:00 PM
In Danny DeVito's
basement

9 A play needs an audience. Put up posters that tell about your play. Don't forget to write the title of the play and the date, time, and place.

10 When it's almost time for the show, set up chairs facing the stage. Ask helpers to show people to their seats.

14

It's show time! Have fun!
And if you make a mistake, don't worry.
Just smile and keep on going.

Congratulations! You did it! While everyone's clapping, don't forget to come back out and take a bow.